Emerald
Isle
Adventures

Emerald Isle
Adventures

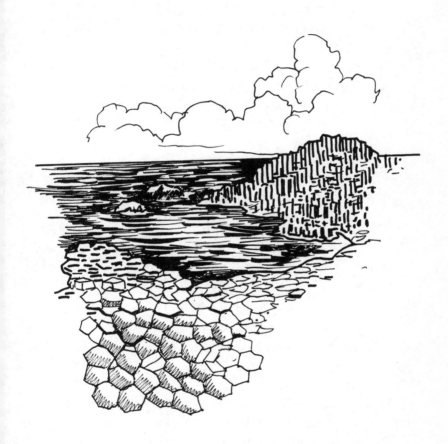

Robert Plant

CF4·K

To my wife Karen and daughter Grace
without whose encouragement and help I would never
have put pen to paper.

10 9 8 7 6 5 4 3 2 1
© Copyright 2013 Robert Plant
ISBN: 978-1-78191-136-5

Published in 2013 by
Christian Focus Publications,
Geanies House, Fearn, Tain,
Ross-shire, IV20 1TW,
Great Britain

Cover design by Daniel van Straaten
Cover illustration by Graham Kennedy
Other illustrations by Graham Kennedy
Printed by Bell and Bain, Glasgow

Contents

Emerald Isle

Ireland – the 'Emerald Isle' – situated off the west coast of Great Britain and covering an area of over 84,000 square kilometres, is one of the most picturesque countries in the world. It has 2,797 kilometres of coastline (not including all its islands) which varies from large sandy beaches and small sheltered bays, to high windswept cliffs, teaming with wildlife. Travelling through Ireland, you will notice that the predominant colour is green, giving rise to its being known around the world as the 'Emerald Isle'.

Did you know that Ireland is the twentieth largest island in the world and the second largest in Europe, after Britain (if you exclude Iceland)? Ireland consists of two countries and thirty-two counties comprising twenty-six in the south, known as the Republic of Ireland and six in the north, known as Northern Ireland or Ulster. Ireland was ruled as part of the United Kingdom until it was partitioned into the north and south in 1922, the south becoming a totally independent nation but the north remaining allied with Great Britain.

Having hundreds of kilometres of coastline, Ireland is greatly influenced by the sea in terms of its wildlife, geography and geology. It is a land of mountains and lochs, rivers and rocks, leprechauns and giants! Ireland also contains one of the most interesting and captivating histories of any land on earth, reaching right back to Norman times.

Have you heard of the term 'The Troubles'? This was a thirty-year period of unrest at the close of the last century, mainly between the Catholic and Protestant communities. They were divided about whether Ireland should remain as two countries or be united as one, under the flag of the southern Republic. Sadly, during this period of upheaval, many hundreds of people died in shootings and bombings, as both sides were guilty of committing the most horrendous atrocities. Thankfully, since what was called the 'Good Friday Agreement' was signed in 1998 and the introduction of the even newer power-sharing executive ruling Northern Ireland from Stormont (its capital building), those sad and deadly days are past.

Today, there are only a few extremists still wanting to resort to violent methods in order to get their way. The legacy of these times, however, continues to live on in many people's minds as they remember terrible news headlines from these dark days. Sadly, most of these people have never visited Ireland and can only associate it with 'The Troubles'. I hope, as you read this book, you will discover what a beautiful and exciting place the Emerald Isle really is.

It is a country which has produced some of the most famous writers, scientists and intellectuals in the world, as well as laying claim to having had twenty-three American Presidents with

Irish ancestry. The grandfather of famous American actress Grace Kelly, who later became Princess of Monaco, was born in Ireland. Once married and known as Princess Grace of Monaco, she made a hobby of collecting Irish books and music. By the time of her untimely death in a car accident in 1981, her library contained over eight thousand titles. This extensive collection can still be seen in her hometown of Monaco, at the Princess Grace Irish Library.

We have included a 'Things to Do and See' section for the majority of the chapters. However, it is worth checking the opening times of these places as they do vary widely.

So, come with me on a journey up high mountains, along winding rivers, through picturesque towns, offshore to isolated islands, and descending deep underground, as well as getting up close and personal with some famous sons and daughters of Ireland.

A Princess in Peril

The last week of January 1953 will be remembered throughout Britain and Ireland as one of the stormiest and wettest ever recorded. The storms caused what came to be known as the 'North Sea Flood' in England. There, the waters of the sea had swept inland over the low lying areas causing severe flooding to large parts of England's east coast, resulting in the death of over five hundred people.

In 1947, the *Princess Victoria* became the first 'roll-on-roll-off' passenger ferry (where vehicles could be driven on and off the ship) to be built and sail in British waters. The ship ran every day between the ports of Stranraer, in Scotland and Larne, in Northern Ireland. The ferry was not large by today's standards but was thought to be revolutionary back in the days following the Second World War. The ship weighed 2,444 tonnes, was 94 metres long, 15 metres wide and had a maximum speed of 19 knots. It was capable of carrying 1500 passengers, 40 cars and had sleeping compartments for 54 people.

On 31st January 1953, the *Princess Victoria* set sail from Stranraer at 7.45 a.m. carrying 128 passengers and a crew of 51. The captain was James Ferguson who, at 55, was vastly experienced, having been in command of various ships sailing this route for almost seventeen years. Despite a severe gale warning being in place, the *Princess Victoria* began her journey to Larne.

After leaving the shelter of Loch Ryan and entering the Irish Sea, the ship was exposed to the full power of the raging winds and mountainous seas. The waves crashing over her stern broke open the 1.52 metre high doors to the car deck, allowing water to flood in, making the ship unstable. Despite the valiant efforts of the crew to fix and secure the damaged doors, over 200 tonnes of water poured in, causing the ship to list to starboard.

Captain Ferguson immediately attempted a return to the relative safety of Loch Ryan. However, in trying to keep the damaged rear of the ship out of the worst of the weather, he found it impossible to manoeuvre safely back towards Stranraer. Approximately two hours after setting sail, the *Princess Victoria* sent out a distress call, stating that she was out of control and required the immediate assistance of tugs to tow her back to port. Three-quarters of an hour later at 10.30 a.m., the *Princess Victoria* sent out her first S.O.S distress message, and a full scale rescue operation began: lifeboats from Portpatrick in Scotland, Donaghadee, in Northern Ireland, as well as Royal Navy ships from Rothesay set sail. An RAF Hastings aircraft flew down towards the scene, leaving another rescue operation in the Western Isles.

Despite the danger she was in, the *Princess Victoria,* by keeping her engines going, drifted further away from the coast of Scotland and closer to the coast of Ireland. The crew, however, continued to send out distress calls, giving the location of the ship as being closer to Scotland. The Royal Navy destroyer, HMS *Contest*, made good time in spite of the severe weather conditions which forced her to slow from 31 knots to 16 knots. Despite this she still managed to cover the 96.6 kilometre distance in just under two-and-a-half hours.

Sadly, most people in the world do not realise that they are in the wrong position with regard to God. The Bible says that 'your iniquities have separated between you and your God, and your sins have hid his face from you, that he will not hear' (Isaiah 59:2). Once we are prepared to acknowledge that we are sinful and separated from God we can turn from our sin and trust his Son, the Lord Jesus, who promises to save all who come to him as Saviour.

Once in the locality provided by the stricken vessel, the *Contest's* crew were unable to see the sinking ship, due to poor visibility and the fact that the *Princess Victoria* had moved from her reported position. At about 1:30 p.m., with her engines now stopped, the crew of the sinking ship sighted the coast of Northern Ireland. They immediately relayed the ship's new location via Morse code [the ship did not have conventional wireless radio communication] to the rescue vessels which were trying desperately to find her. Just before 2.00 p.m., the final message was relayed, confirming that the ship was now sinking and that the order to abandon ship had been given.

Once the *Princess Victoria* had established her position, being close to the mouth of Belfast Lough rather than in Scottish waters, four ships, which had been sheltering from the raging storm in the Lough, immediately put to sea in an attempt to assist in the rescue effort.

However, the strong winds and giant waves proved too much for the ferry and the *Princess Victoria* foundered at around 2.00 p.m.

The continuing severity of the storm, meant that when the rescue ships finally arrived, they were unable to lift the survivors from the lifeboats. The ships positioned themselves around the lifeboats providing some protection from the fierce storm and mountainous seas. Eventually, the Donaghadee lifeboat, called *Sir Samuel Kelly*, arrived on the scene and was able to pluck the fortunate survivors from the lifeboats.

The disaster claimed the lives of 133 people, including all the officers of the ship. The captain, James Ferguson, was observed by some survivors standing to attention and saluting as his ship sank beneath him. Forty-four survivors were rescued from the lifeboats which had been launched but, tragically, not a single woman or child survived. The radio operator, David Broadfoot,

was awarded the George Cross, the highest civilian award for bravery, for staying at his post until the ship sank, in a desperate attempt to relay help to the stricken vessel.

Many questions were asked in the weeks and months following the disaster. Why had the ship sailed into such a gale in the first place, why had the stern doors not been strong enough or high enough to withstand the storm and why had the *Princess Victoria* continued to provide wrong information about her location?

We can all learn an important lesson from this disaster. Sin, the wrong things we all do, is like a storm in our lives. The greatest danger that sin brings is that it will keep us out of heaven forever. We need to make sure that we have a Saviour who can save us from this tragedy. God's Word, the Bible, points us to the Lord

Jesus who is the only one who can rescue us and give us a great and wonderful hope of a home in heaven.

On one occasion, the Lord's disciples were in a small boat, in the middle of a great storm, when the Lord came to them, walking upon the water. Peter, wanting to do the same as the Lord climbed out of the small boat and began to walk on the water towards him. However, something happened and poor Peter began to sink down into the water crying out: 'Lord save me' (Matthew 14:30). Immediately, the strong arm of the Lord Jesus Christ reached down and lifted Peter out of the waves. In the same way, when we call upon the Lord, realising the awful danger we are in because of our sin, the Lord will save us and make us fit for heaven. The Bible says: 'Whosoever shall call upon the name of the Lord shall be saved' (Romans 10:13).

THINGS TO SEE AND DO:

- *Princess Victoria* Memorial Cairn – Agnew Park – Stranraer, Scotland.
- *Princess Victoria* Memorial Monument – Bay Road – Larne.
- Ulster Folk and Transport Museum – Can be found just off the A2 Belfast Bangor Road at Holywood. The lifeboat *Sir Samuel Kelly* is on display here, as is a model of the *Princess Victoria*.

Flight into History

If you travel to Errislannan Hill near Clifden in County Galway, you will discover a monument that looks very much like the tail fin of an aircraft. This was placed here on 15th June 1959, to commemorate the fortieth anniversary of the first transatlantic flight which, having left from St. John's in Newfoundland, landed in a bog, around two kilometres south of this point.

John Alcock, from England and Arthur Brown, from Scotland, set off on 14th June 1919, in order to attempt to become the first men to cross the Atlantic Ocean in an aeroplane. Six years previously, the Daily Mail newspaper had offered a prize of £10,000 to the first person to fly from America, Canada or Newfoundland to either Britain or Ireland within seventy-two hours. The two airmen, flying a World War One twin engine Vickers Vimy biplane bomber, sought to be the first to accomplish this feat and claim the prize money.

The 3,042 kilometre flight was far from easy, as the two gallant men fought adverse weather in the form of fog, ice and snow in their attempt to accomplish their goal. Alcock, the pilot, fought to keep the plane airborne, as the Vimy's two Rolls Royce

15

Eagle engines gave him trouble and the aircraft's wings and air intakes kept freezing up. Brown, time and again, left the relative security of the plane's open cockpit to make the perilous walk out across the wings, so as to remove the ice and snow which threatened to make the aircraft too heavy to fly and plunge it into the vast Atlantic Ocean below. Due to the varying weather conditions he experienced, Alcock had to alternate height; on some occasions flying just above the waves, on others having to climb to a maximum of 3,658 metres.

At around 8.40 a.m., on 15th June 1919, Alcock attempted to land the plane on what, due to poor visibility, he thought was a field but was, in actual fact, a bog on the Derrygimlagh Moor. Despite frantic calls and warnings from workers on the ground, whom the airmen thought were merely waving, Alcock landed the Vimy in the bog. The aircraft naturally came to a sudden stop in a nose down position, causing severe damage to it. Thankfully, neither airman was injured in the unorthodox landing and soon the news was out that the two had managed to conquer another mighty chapter in the field of aviation.

The rewards were great: in addition to the prize money, a month later, both men received knighthoods from King George V at Buckingham Palace. Sadly, John Alcock did not live long to enjoy the recognition he had earned, as he was killed later that year on 18th December, whilst en-route to the Paris Air Show, in a Vickers Viking.

Wherever there are challenges, people will rise to them. *The Guinness Book of Records* is full of such accomplishments. The Christian life is no different, as those who have repented of their sins and taken Christ as Saviour, seek to live for him in a dangerous and difficult world. Often, as we live for God, we will have to rise up and make a stand, even when we may become unpopular with friends because we are not happy with things they wish to do or be involved in. The Christian life is not easy but the Bible does give some good advice when it says: 'Seek those things which are above, where Christ sitteth on the right hand of God' (Colossians 3:1). This means we need to read our Bibles and pray every day and do the things which will keep us close to God and the Lord Jesus like regularly meeting with other Bible-believing Christians. That way we can be assured of victory when trials come upon us.

Alcock and Brown were not the only ones to fly into history in Ireland: ten years before, in 1909, a twenty-five-year-old inventor by the name of Harry Ferguson, became the first person to fly an aeroplane over Ireland. Having been impressed by the Wright brothers' first manned flight in 1903, the young Harry was determined to fly himself. He worked steadily on building a plane throughout the year 1909 until, in December, it was finally ready. He took it to Hillsborough Park where, after a failed attempt owing to bad weather, Harry managed to get airborne on the last day of the year and fly the great length of 119 metres before crash landing in a cornfield!

The next year, Harry was busy again, this time taking his plane to County Down where, in August, he managed to fly five kilometres from Dundrum to Newcastle, winning himself the grand sum of £100 prize money offered by the town of Newcastle! Ferguson, however, did not stop here: he went on to design and build a completely new type of tractor with a totally unique linkage system that allowed different tools to be easily attached. This 'Little Grey Fergie', as it came to be known, would revolutionise farming all over the world. The now famous brand of Massey Ferguson was born.

THINGS TO SEE AND DO:

- White Memorial Cairn on the spot where a Marconi wireless station stood, from which Alcock and Brown first transmitted news of their success. This is situated about 500 m from their landing spot and 4 km south of Clifden in County Galway.
- Aircraft Tailfin Monument on Errislannan Hill, 2 km north of their landing site, which was set up on the 40th anniversary of the landing, on 15th June 1959.
- London – London Science Museum - Alcock and Brown's rebuilt aircraft is on display here.
- Newcastle, County Down – Granite stone plaque on the Promenade recognises Harry Ferguson's three mile flight in 1910.

Tales of Narnia

If you have read about Peter, Edmund, Susan and Lucy and their adventures in Narnia, you will already be acquainted with some of the best children's stories ever written. However, just how much do you know about the author of the Narnia series? Well, welcome to the magical world of Clive Staples Lewis. C. S. Lewis was born on 29th November 1898 in Belfast. He was known to his friends and family as 'Jack', a name he coined for himself after a beloved neighbourhood dog called 'Jacksie' died. Lewis' mother passed away in 1908 when he was just nine years old and in 1910 Lewis became a boarding student at Campbell College, Belfast, only staying there a year before moving to Malvern College, England. During the First World War, Lewis was involved in action in the trenches of the Somme where, in April 1918, he was wounded by a British shell which fell short of its target. Thankfully, he recovered from his injuries and following the end of The First World War Lewis became a tutor in English Literature at Oxford University.

Having rejected Christianity in his teenage years, Lewis was brought face to face with his need of salvation on many occasions. At the age of thirty-two, after many years of persuading and conviction, Lewis recorded trusting the Lord Jesus Christ as his Saviour. He did not make this decision easily, and something of the difficulties he faced in getting right with God he later recounted in a book he wrote titled *Surprised by Joy*.

Many people reject God's Word, the Bible, without having honestly considered its wonderful message or its claims to be inspired by God! Some people in the world today will say that God does not exist. However, God says, 'The fool hath said in his heart there is no God' (Psalm 14:1). We need to be very serious when it comes to our thoughts of and about God as one day we will meet him and have to give an account of why we rejected him and his offer of salvation. We need, like C. S. Lewis,

to stop rejecting the Lord Jesus but accept him as Saviour for he says 'Come unto me … and I will give you rest' (Matthew 11:28).

It was in 1949 that C. S. Lewis commenced writing his books called *The Chronicles of Narnia*. In these, he depicts the fight between good and evil, the great Lion, Aslan, being the central character. The series of seven fantasy novels for children were completed in 1954 and Lewis said that his ideas for the land of Narnia came from his love for the Mountains of Mourne. The books were so successful that 100 million copies have been sold and they have been translated into over forty different languages, as well as being made into several radio and TV productions and a few full-length feature films.

These wonderfully exciting stories have Peter, Edmund, Susan and Lucy mysteriously transported to the Land of Narnia through the back of their uncle's wardrobe. Once in Narnia they battle

witches, beasts and other powers with the help of their friend and guardian, Aslan the Lion. Lewis based his adventures on various Bible stories, including the death, burial and resurrection of the Lord Jesus which he used as his basis for the death and resurrection of Aslan, the great Lion, who came back to life after being killed by the white witch.

Although primarily remembered for these great works of fiction, C. S. Lewis wrote many other books, which are well worth reading.

C. S. Lewis died exactly one week before his 65th birthday, on 22nd November 1963, the very same day on which the United States President, John F. Kennedy, was assassinated. Sadly, Lewis's death was overlooked in some newspapers of the time, due to the greater headline news of the president's death.

Although a wonderfully gifted storyteller, C. S. Lewis could never rival the wonderful true story of the Bible, the Word of God. This tells of God's great love for sinners and his willingness to send his own Son, the Lord Jesus, into the world to die so that we can be forgiven. The message is summed up in these wonderful words: 'For God so loved the world, that he gave his only begotten Son, that whosoever believeth in him should not perish, but have everlasting life' (John 3:16).

THINGS TO SEE AND DO:

- Linen Hall Library, 17 Donegal Square North, Belfast BT1 5GB, houses a unique collection of books both by and about Lewis.
- Holywood Arches Library, Holywood Road, Belfast – full size statue of C. S. Lewis entering into the wardrobe that leads to the land of Narnia.

The Divided City

Any trip to Ireland could not be complete without a visit to Dublin, the capital of Southern Ireland. Dublin is a vast city with a population of half a million in the centre and over one million, taking in all its suburbs.

As in all major cities, there is a thriving shopping and entertainment centre, as well as Croke Park, home to the Gaelic Football Association, ranked as Europe's third largest sports stadium with a capacity of over 82,000 people. There is also a second great sports stadium in the city, formally known as Lansdowne Road. Following a huge multimillion pound upgrade, it changed its name to the Aviva Stadium, which has an all-seating capacity of 50,000. This stadium is the home of the Irish Rugby Football Union; however, the national Republic of Ireland football team also play their home matches at this venue.

The city of Dublin is divided into two: the north side and the south side by the River Liffey. Both sides of the river have traditionally been different: the north side is considered to be working class; the south side more middle or even upper class.

Whilst visiting Dublin, a trip to Kilmainham Gaol is a must. In this now disused prison, you can explore the cells that once held prisoners of all types between its opening in 1726 and its closure, in 1924. Here, Eamon DeValera, third president of Ireland from 1959 to 1973, was held, following what has come to be known as 'The Easter Rising' in 1916. This was an occasion when native Irishmen sought to overthrow English rule.

After a week, the rising was put down and the ringleaders arrested and eventually executed. DeValera was spared due, in large measure, to the fact that he was born in America and the British, who were at the time fighting Germany during the First World War, did not want to upset their American cousins! Wander through these cold dark stone walls and try to imagine the grim life you would have had here as a prisoner all those years ago.

How wonderful it is to know that God does not divide us into nations, categories, castes or peoples, according to our place of birth or standing in life. He does, however, state that 'All have sinned' (Romans 3:23) and that: 'All the world.... may become guilty before God' (Romans 3:19). As a result of our sin and guilt, there is a division between us and God which only God can fix. That is why he sent his Son the Lord Jesus: 'To be the Saviour of the World' (1 John 4:14). If we are prepared to be really sorry for the wrong things that we do in our lives, which the Bible calls sins, by asking God to forgive us and trusting the Lord Jesus as our Saviour, he can cleanse us and remove this terrible division making us right with God and fit for heaven.

Bridges Across Troubled Waters

If you ever travel to the beautiful and spectacular North Antrim coast in Northern Ireland, you will, I believe, want to cross the sea to the small island of Carrick. In order to do this, you will either need to go by boat, helicopter or, more easily, by the unusual bridge that links this tiny island with the mainland. Be warned, however, before you cross, that some visitors to this interesting and unique attraction have had to be taken off Carrick Island by boat, as they have been too scared to walk back across the bridge! The amazing thing about the world famous Carrick-a-Rede Bridge is, that it is a suspension bridge made from rope, which spans a gap of 20 metres and hangs 30 metres above the sea below.

A bridge of varying proportions has connected the island since the 1600s to allow fishermen onto Carrick, in order to fish for salmon which return to breed along the Bann and Bush Rivers. Strange to relate, that in all the years the bridge has been in use, there are no recorded accidents of people falling off the often rather precarious crossing! The actual name, Carrick-a-Rede, means 'rock in the road' and may refer to the jagged rocks, which can be seen below the bridge at low tide.

It is always a bit of an adventure to walk across the Carrick-a-Rede Bridge but perhaps slightly more interesting when the wind is blowing and the bridge is swinging a bit. If you ever cross it in these conditions, just imagine what the bridge was like about forty years ago, when it only had a rope handrail on one side of it!

Another bridge that is well worth crossing is the Broadmeadow Viaduct, which spans the Broadmeadow Estuary, between Malahide and Donabate, north of Dublin. If, however, you do decide to visit this bridge, you will need to catch a train to negotiate its 176 metre length, successfully. This Victorian structure, commenced in 1860, carries the main Dublin-Belfast railway line and is therefore used by many trains each day.

On the evening of Friday 21st August 2009, a 20 metre section of the bridge fell into the water below, leaving the railway line suspended. This incident happened just seconds after a train had passed over it. The driver of this train had observed the track undulating and part of the structure crumbling away. He was hailed as a hero after stopping his train at Malahide in order to report what he had observed, as any other trains passing across the bridge would undoubtedly have ended up in the waters of the estuary, causing great loss of life.

If you take a visit to Dublin, you will find much interest in crossing the River Liffey on the old pedestrian Ha'penny Bridge. This beautiful ancient bridge was opened in 1816 and called the Wellington Bridge, to mark the great victory of the Duke of Wellington over his French enemy Napoleon Bonaparte at the battle of Waterloo the previous year. The price or toll to cross the bridge was one halfpenny; hence, over time, the name was changed to the Ha'penny Bridge. This was, in fact, the only pedestrian bridge across the river in Dublin, until the new Millennial Bridge was opened in the year 2000.

How wonderful to know, that through the love and mercy of God, there is a 'bridge to everlasting life', provided by the Lord Jesus Christ. By His death on the cross and resurrection from the dead, he has spanned the gulf of our sin which separates people from God and made it possible for us to be ready for heaven. The

Bible says that: 'There is One God, and One mediator between God and men, the man Christ Jesus' (1 Timothy 2:5). If we are prepared to trust him as Saviour we can cross from the death of sin to eternal life, by his Bridge.

A trip to Galway should take in the strangely named village of O'Brien's Bridge, situated on the River Shannon. A bridge has spanned the river here since 1506, when the family of Brian Boru (King of Munster and first king of Ireland from 1001 to 1014) built a simple wooden crossing, which lasted for four years before being burned down during a local dispute. This was replaced by an impressive stone structure with towers and twelve-foot thick walls.

This crossing lasted for twenty-five years, until Henry VIII ordered its destruction in 1537, in response to a rebellion against the English king. The O'Brien family constructed a third crossing at the same site and this bridge still stands today.

THINGS TO SEE AND DO:
- Carrick-a-Rede rope bridge, Balintoy, Co Antrim. Owned by National Trust. You need to walk about half a mile from the car park to the bridge itself.
- Ha'penny Bridge. Crossing the River Liffey between Lower Ormond Quay and Wellington Quay, found at the south end of Lower Liffey Street.

A Hole in the Door

Old buildings often tend to be interesting, but old buildings with real live history contained within them are, of course, fascinating! A visit to St Patrick's Cathedral in Dublin should excite you, as you gaze at its splendid architecture, life-like statues, imposing roof lines and the 43 metre high tower. Recorded within its walls, was a most unusual event, which resulted in the introduction of a worldwide figure of speech.

St Patrick's Cathedral, the largest church building in Ireland, was commenced in the 1200s and totally renovated during the closing years of the 1800s. Originally, it was built to commemorate the visit of the patron saint of Ireland, St Patrick, whom it is suggested, baptised converts to Christianity near the site. If you have ever read the story or seen the film about 'Gulliver's Travels', you may be interested to know that the book's author, Jonathan Swift, was the dean of the cathedral from 1713 to 1745.

A must see attraction in the cathedral is what is known as the 'Door of Reconciliation', the history of which goes back to the year 1492. Two of Ireland's leading noble families at the time, the FitzGeralds, who were the Earls of Kildare and the Butlers who were Earls of Ormond, had a rather long-running dispute between them. The nephew of the Earl of Ormond, called Black James, was fleeing from the soldiers of the FitzGerald family, under the command of Gerald Gearoid Mor FitzGerald, the 8th Earl of Kildare, sometimes referred to as 'Garret the Great'.

Black James and his soldiers eventually found safety in the Chapter House of St Patrick's Cathedral and, although totally surrounded by the FitzGerald army, refused to give up the safety of the Chapter House. Eventually, Gerald FitzGerald ordered his soldiers to cut a rectangular hole in the centre of the Chapter House door. This done, he began to negotiate with Black James, seeking peace between the two families. Finally, he thrust his arm in through the door in order to shake the hand of his former enemy and to bring to an end the family feud.

This was a surprising move by the Earl of Kildare as, at that time, he was the Lord Deputy of Ireland and known to rule with a 'rod of iron'. It could also have been a fatal decision, as Black James could have had one of his soldiers cut off the prone arm of his enemy! He took, however, the proffered hand and brought the long-running family dispute to an end. From that time on, the door became known as the 'Door of Reconciliation' and, although the Chapter House in which the incident took place has long since gone, the door is on display along with its hole, in the main cathedral.

At sometime in your life, you may be asked to 'chance your arm'. The expression means to take a risk in some way and comes directly from this incident involving two warring families.

It was a gracious and kind act Gerald FitzGerald made to Black James when his men had his enemy surrounded and he could easily have brought the dispute to a more deadly end. And yet in some small way this pictures the wonderful Bible truth of reconciliation, as the Bible states that: 'God was in Christ, reconciling the world unto himself' (2 Corinthians 5:19). God sent his Son, the Lord Jesus, in order to reconcile (bring together) us, the sinful ones, and God, the holy and sinless. The Lord Jesus made this possible by being made sin when he was on the cross, taking the punishment our sins deserved. If we are prepared to trust the Lord Jesus, we can be brought into God's family, having been reconciled to God by his Son.

THINGS TO SEE AND DO:
- St Patrick's Cathedral, Saint Patrick's Close, Dublin 8.

Pirates of the Elizabethan

Maybe you are one of those people enthralled by the adventures of pirates of the past. Do you enjoy reading the stories of how they captured other people's treasures, or made their enemies walk the plank to drop off into a watery grave? Maybe, too, some of the modern pirate films have caught your attention with their sword fights and constant edge-of-the-seat excitement. I am sure there cannot be too many pirates in history who have been entertained by the Queen of England in order to seek their co-operation. There is one, however, who came from Ireland and, perhaps most surprisingly of all, this pirate was a lady! Meet Grace O'Malley!

It is not certain when Grace was born but popular belief is that it was during the reign of King Henry VIII, possibly in the year 1530, at Clew Bay, County Mayo on the West Coast of Ireland [although she made Clare Island just outside the bay her home for much of her life].

Her father, Eoghan, was the chief of the O'Malley clan, who taxed all who lived within the confines of their land, as well as those who fished the seas off the coast of Clew Bay. He often went on trading expeditions and (so tradition records) Grace (aged 13) wanting to accompany him on a trip to Spain, cut off her hair so as to look more like a male sailor, thus causing her father to accept her as one of the crew.

When her father died, Grace, inheriting the position of clan chief, hit upon the idea of demanding taxes, not just from those on her land but from ships passing close to her island home. Having gained the support of over 200 men, she was not without power! She and her ship or ships sailed swiftly out to meet passing merchant schooners, which were boarded and taxes demanded either in cash or part of its cargo.

News spread quickly of Grace O'Malley's escapades but, due to her incredible knowledge of the west Ireland coastline, she and her followers were able to escape quickly from the scene of their crimes amongst the plentiful islands and coves in that area.

Eventually, in 1577, the law caught up with Grace and she was arrested, tried and imprisoned in Limerick castle. Following her release, she went back to the life of a pirate. Amazingly, Queen Elizabeth I, totally fed up with reports of Grace's constant attacks on British ships, called Grace to London to meet her. Grace duly obliged and, as neither spoke the other's language, a deal was struck through interpreters whereby Grace agreed not to interfere with ships flying British flags. Grace kept to her word for a number of years, before finally going back to her old ways and, once again, stopping and 'taxing' British ships, right up until her death in 1603.

Most of us would consider it a great privilege to be called to speak to a king or queen. The Bible warns each of us, that we need to be prepared to meet God. 'Every one of us shall give account of himself to God' (Romans 14:12). Wouldn't you love to know what Queen Elizabeth had to say to Pirate Grace at their meeting? I wonder, however, what we will have to confess to God, when we meet him and what God will say to us about how we have lived. We need to be ready for that meeting and the Bible says that the only one who can make us ready, is God's Son, the Lord Jesus. If he is our Saviour, we need not ever fear meeting God for we can say with the apostle Paul in the Bible 'We have peace with God through our Lord Jesus Christ' (Romans 5:1).

There was, amazingly, an even more famous Irish woman pirate, by the name of Anne Bonny. Anne was apparently born in Kinsale, County Cork around 1700 but, after the family moved to America, she ran away from home in her teens to marry and sail with a peasant sailor. Soon, however, Anne grew increasingly

bored with life, until she met the swashbuckling Calico Jack Rackham who stole her heart. Hardly surprising as he was a pirate and liked to steal things belonging to other people!

Once together, they stopped, plundered and stole from ships all around the Caribbean, amassing a large amount of stolen bounty as a result. Anne had also engaged the services of another female pirate named Mary Read. The British Navy, however, was hot on their trail and, in October 1720, all three were captured after a fierce fight, in which brave Calico Jack could not take part due to being drunk.

Anne was asked to testify at Jack's trial but, being so incensed with his failure to fight, she answered: 'If he had fought like a man, he need not have been hanged like a dog'. After the trial, Jack was sentenced to hang and executed.

At the trial of Anne and Mary, much evidence was heard about their cut-throat exploits, with both gun and sword. Both women were also given the death penalty for their many crimes. Upon hearing the guilty verdict, however, both girls declared they were expecting children. The law at the time did not allow women who were pregnant to be hung, so both were temporarily reprieved. Mary died soon afterwards in prison, due to a fever, but Anne apparently gave birth to a baby after which, sadly, she disappears from history.

A Politician Returns

On 26th June 1963, President John F. Kennedy, the thirty-fifth president of America and great-grandson of an Irish immigrant, landed in Ireland, on a four-day visit. This would include trips to Dublin, Wexford, Cork, Galway and Limerick! He landed in Dublin on board the first purpose-built aircraft for carrying United States presidents, which was being used on its first international trip – 'Air Force One'.

Earlier on that day, the President had addressed a large crowd in Berlin, as he looked over the infamous Berlin Wall which at that time separated East and West Berlin. Here he made a very famous speech stating in German 'Ich bin ein Berliner' (I am a Berliner). This speech has been recorded as one of the most famous political speeches of the 20th century!

The next day, President Kennedy travelled south to the small village of Dunganstown, Co Wexford to meet his relatives, in particular his cousin Mary Kennedy Ryan and her daughters. It was here in the farmyard of his ancestral home that Mr Kennedy partook of home-made bread, salmon sandwiches and tea (with two sugars) surrounded by villagers, reporters and his own personnel, who had travelled with him from America.

Later, John F. Kennedy travelled the short distance to Wexford, to find all the local businesses had shut down for the day in his honour and 50,000 people were waiting to hear his speech. You can retrace President Kennedy's visit and life by visiting the Kennedy family homestead.

Two days later, the president was flown to the town of Galway, where an estimated 100,000 people were waiting to welcome him. He stood up in his open car, as it passed the massive crowds, so that he could shake the hands of so many that had turned out to meet him. He gave a speech in Eyre square, which would later be renamed the 'Kennedy Memorial Park' in his honour.

I guess we all like to receive a warm welcome whenever we return home. It is nice to feel wanted and appreciated. The Lord Jesus told a story of a young man who was desperate to leave home but, in doing so, wasted his time, money and life in worldly pursuits. Once he realised his mistake, he returned home a desperate person, not knowing quite how his father or family would receive him. But what a welcome was waiting for him! 'When he was yet a great way off, his father saw him, and had compassion, and ran, and fell on his neck, and kissed him' (Luke 15:20). The Lord told this story to show us, that although our sins keep us far from God, when we repent of our wrongdoings and return in humility to God by trusting his Son as Saviour, God is willing to forgive and welcome us into his family.

The rest of the manic four-day tour of Ireland was seen by all as a great success and is still talked about with enthusiasm. Sadly, just five months after President Kennedy's visit to Ireland, he was killed by an assassin's bullet as he drove through Dallas, Texas, on Friday 22nd November 1963!

Also worth a visit is the Kennedy Arboretum, situated in nearby New Ross. This is a 600 acre wooded area containing many types of trees, hedges and plants, funded as a memorial to the fallen President by a wealthy American with Irish ancestry.

THINGS TO SEE AND DO:
- Kennedy Homestead, just off the B733 in New Ross, Co Wexford. Here you can be given a guided tour around the homestead by one of the Kennedy family!
- Kennedy Memorial Park, Eyre Square, Galway. This is the place in Galway where President Kennedy addressed a crowd of over 100,000 people, on Saturday, 29th June 1963.

Is it Football or Rugby or ...?

Okay, ready for a really difficult sporting challenge? Name a game in which you can score points like rugby, by kicking or even hitting the ball over a cross bar and between two upright posts; or score a goal, as in football, by kicking the ball into a netted goal, in which you not only score a goal but a goal equalling three points! Confused? Well, welcome to Gaelic football!

Gaelic football is played on a rectangular pitch, marked out in a similar style to a rugby pitch, although of a much larger size. The two teams consist of fifteen players and up to fifteen substitutes (although only five substitutions are allowed each game). Most matches last for an hour with a fifteen-minute half-time break, after thirty minutes of play.

Although, perhaps, the game is more like rugby than football, the ball used is actually round and similar in size and weight to that of a volley ball. The goals bear similarities to rugby posts, with the upright bars at the top. The bottom of the bar, however, has a net similar to a football goal. You can score by either getting the ball between two upright posts to gain one point or, a more conventional football-type goal, by striking the ball into the net. This is called a goal and is worth three points. The tackling of an opponent in order to obtain the ball is, once again, something of a cross between conventional football and rugby, in which shoulder charging or knocking the ball out of an opponent's hands is allowed but any rougher contact becomes a foul!

The game has many rules and regulations that are peculiar to its own way of playing. These include not only having a referee and linesmen but also the provision of four umpires, two at either end of the field, who are there primarily to judge the scoring of points or goals. They decide whether the shot was wide, high or should be disallowed. The extra officials, unlike their counterparts in more conventional games, have no power to intervene if a foul has been committed or unfair play has been witnessed. All these decisions are the sole responsibility of the referee.

Surprisingly, Gaelic football is claimed to be one of the oldest forms of sport in the world, dating back to the 1300s. However, it was around 1670 that the game, as it is played nowadays, was fully recognised. There are also, today, many female teams around Ireland, establishing the game's popularity among both male and female participants.

Maybe you feel that Gaelic football is not for you? Well, why not try hurling? Actually, the two games have much in common, both being played on the same field, using the same scoring system, both having the same length of play and number of

players! It is claimed that the game of hurling had been played in Ireland for the past 2,000 years, or more. However, in modern times, innovations were introduced to make the game safer. These include helmets, shin pads and gloves!

In hurling, players use a wooden stick called a 'hurley', which looks a bit like a giant wooden spoon and ranges between around 70 centimetres and one metre in length. This is used in order to hit a small ball called a 'sliotar' which has a cork centre, leather cover and a circumference of around 25 centimetres, although this can vary. The 'hurley' used by the goalkeeper usually has a larger end, which is used by him to try and protect his goal. The ball can be carried (for not more than four steps), hit on the ground or in the air, slapped or kicked towards other team mates or the opponent's goal. If a player wants to carry the ball further than four steps, he has to either balance it on the end of his 'hurley' or bounce it. Players are not allowed to pick the ball directly up off the ground so they have to flick it up either with their hurley or their feet. You are not allowed to throw the sliotar in order to pass it, so you have to slap it with the open hand.

Strangely enough, the Bible uses many sporting illustrations, especially in the New Testament, in order to give examples of its truth. The apostle Paul uses the illustration of the runner: 'Know ye not that they which run in a race run all, but one receiveth the prize? So run, that ye may obtain' (1 Corinthians 9:24). Paul is trying to show that, just as a runner in a race participates in order to do his very best and win to receive the gold medal, so those who belong to the Lord Jesus, should think in a similar way. As we live and work for him, we should always do the very best we can whether it be at school, university or work. Then, at the day when our lives and service will be reviewed by him in Heaven, we will receive a worthy reward from the Lord Jesus for being faithful. How are you running your Christian race?

THINGS TO SEE AND DO:
- Croke Park Stadium and GAA Museum, Cushack Stand, St Joseph's Avenue, Croke Park, Dublin 3. Here you can take a tour of the Stadium, as well as see the GAA (Gaelic Athletic Association) Museum where you can learn more about Gaelic sports. There is also an interesting shop.

Ships, Seafaring and Shipwrecks

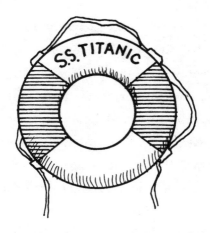

Have you heard of the *Titanic*? I think that perhaps it is the most famous ship in the world, due to the fact that it struck an iceberg and sank on its very first voyage. Well, the *Titanic*, along with its slightly less famous sister ships, *Olympic* and *Britannic*, was built at the Harland and Wolf shipyards in Belfast. As you travel round the city of Belfast, you can easily see the shipyards in the docks area from many vantage points, as they are dwarfed by two giant yellow cranes nicknamed after two Bible characters 'Samson' and 'Goliath'. It was here, in what is now called the 'Titanic Quarter' of the city, that the great and beautiful *Titanic*, the world's most famous ship was built.

The *Titanic* was launched on 31st May 1911 and spent nearly a year being fitted with all the latest luxury furnishings of its day. On 2nd April 1912 it took its sea trials in Belfast Lough and was pronounced safe and ready to sail. At 8 p.m. that night the *Titanic* left Belfast for the first and last time to sail to Southampton, before making what was to be its tragic maiden voyage across the Atlantic Ocean. It actually did stop again in Ireland, at Queenstown (now named Cobh) in order to pick up some Irish emigrants and mail, before steaming west and into history.

Another famous ship, the *Lusitania*, was launched in 1905 and was, in its day, one of the biggest and grandest ships afloat. During its career it won the prestigious 'Blue Ribbon' award on several occasions for having the fastest time in crossing the Atlantic Ocean from Britain to America.

The First World War had commenced on 28th July 1914 and, on 22nd April 191 the German government issued a notice warning passengers in America, travelling to the United Kingdom, that they would be legitimate targets of the German navy once within British waters. On 7th May 1915 the *Lusitania* was spotted by a German U-Boat, named *UB-20*, around 16 kilometres off the Old Head of Kinsale on the southwest coast of Ireland and torpedoed. The ship took a direct hit just below the bridge area and began to list heavily to starboard. The *Lusitania* took just

eighteen minutes to sink in 92 metres of water, taking nearly 1,200 passengers and crew with her to a watery grave. This single act by Germany brought international condemnation from around the world and led directly to America entering the war allied to Britain and France.

If you travel to the Giant's Causeway on the north Antrim coast and walk a little in an easterly direction, you will come to a bay called Port na Spaniagh. It was here in the year 1588 that the *Girona* was wrecked, with the loss of well over a thousand Spanish soldiers and sailors. The *Girona* was a warship belonging to the Spanish navy, which had been part of the great Armada sent to invade Great Britain. Due, however, to the great seamanship of Sir Francis Drake and the combined forces of nature, the Armada failed in its mission. The *Girona* had been blown right around the west coast of Ireland and was heading for what it believed to be the relative safety of Dunluce Castle before sailing across to Scotland. Sadly, for all on board, the ship approached

land during a storm several kilometres further east than intended, wrecking itself on the deadly rocks just under the surface.

Those few who managed to get through the swirling surf to the shore were faced with another deadly danger in the form of unfriendly locals. Some did survive and there are families in that area even today who claim to be descendents of some of those who sailed on the *Girona*. Over the years much gold was plundered from the remains of the ship which lay in shallow water, some even being used to pay for extensions and renovations to Dunluce Castle.

Another couple of bays further round the coast heading towards the little harbour of Dunseverick, will bring you to a sheltered cove, which was used during the Second World War to harbour a German submarine for several hours. The crew of the U-Boat had run out of fresh water supplies and so, in order to avoid possible dehydration and disease, the captain made the daring decision to put ashore on Ireland's north coast to replenish his water supplies.

Many locals looking down from the safety of the cliff tops were able to observe the submarine and its crew, as they collected water from a nearby waterfall and brought it back to the vessel. Despite the Allied authorities being informed about the submarine's daring landing, they were unable to do anything to stop the vessel and crew before they were long gone.

The apostle Paul was inspired by God to write nearly half of our New Testament. In one of his letters to Christians in a town called Corinth, he said that, on three occasions, he had suffered being shipwrecked and, in one of those incidents, he had spent a whole night and day in the sea waiting to be rescued. Sometimes being a Christian is not easy. It can often be very hard.

On one of those shipwreck occasions that we read of in the book of Acts, Paul, although a Roman prisoner for his faith in the Lord Jesus, stood and warned that if the ship set sail it would be in great danger. Sadly, of course, no one believed him and, despite his warnings, the ship ran into a terrible gale. In the midst of this storm, Paul boldly stood and said 'I believe God' (Acts 27:25). The ship was wrecked. However, this time, because the passengers and crew had taken Paul's advice, no one was lost. If you have been saved and are therefore a Christian, maybe the Lord could use you to see souls saved, just by being prepared to say: 'I believe God' and making a stand for the Lord Jesus, even despite the hardships and storms your actions might bring about.

THINGS TO SEE AND DO:

- Titanic Belfast Museum, Titanic Quarter, Belfast – This fantastic £100 million pound museum resembling four ships' bows, is built overlooking the slipway, where the *Titanic* was built and contains many artefacts from the ship and those who travelled on her.
- Ulster Folk and Transport Museum – just off the A2 Belfast Bangor Road at Holywood, contains a *Titanic* exhibition, amongst other interesting facts and exhibits.
- *Lusitania* Memorial, Casement Square, Cobh, County Cork. This is a memorial statue erected to remember the victims of the disaster, which took place just off the coast of the town.

Moonscapes and Moher

There is no doubt that Ireland boasts some of the most outstanding and majestic natural history in the world. Right across this amazing island, you will come face to face with nature in all its beauty, diversity and breathtaking wonder.

Go west to the coast of the pretty County Clare and you will discover the mighty Cliffs of Moher. These soaring cliffs have been weathered out of black shale and sandstone over hundreds of years. They stretch for nearly 8 kilometres along Ireland's western seaboard and rise in height to 214 metres. At the bottom, they are battered by the relentless pounding of the Atlantic Ocean whilst, at the top, is the emerald green of the spongy grassland. These cliffs are home to over 30,000 seabirds with around twenty different species nesting in their rocky crags, making them a birdwatcher's delight!

Almost halfway along, standing at the cliffs highest point, is O'Briens Tower. This building was constructed in 1835 by

Cornelius O'Brien as an observation post, allegedly to provide better views for the many visitors who came to the cliffs. From the top of the tower it is possible to see a wonderful panorama in any direction – stunning on a clear day! As the sun sets on the western horizon, these magnificent cliffs turn an almost russet red colour, further enhancing their already spectacular appearance.

Not far from the Cliffs of Moher, you will come across the rather more tranquil but no less impressive limestone region known as the Burren. The name 'Burren' simply means rocky land and here you will discover 40,000 acres of it! This marvellous limestone pavement is the closest that you will get to walking on the moon, in Ireland! Here you will find contorted rocks, weathered limestone and rounded hillocks which, in winter, display an almost unearthly barrenness, but in summer come alive with colours from the many hardy wildflowers which inhabit the region.

A strange almost mystical phenomenon in the Burren, is the sudden appearance or disappearance of ponds of water. As you walk across this barren limestone wilderness, you may notice that ponds which you passed earlier, have mysteriously disappeared or that areas over which you have previously walked, are now flooded with water! Below your feet is an unseen but complex cave system through which water pours continuously. Once these caves flood, the excess water is forced up through holes in the rocks' surface called grykes, forming almost instantaneously the surface ponds. When the water level below ground drops, the ponds once again disappear into the limestone landscape!

Here too, you will come across some of Ireland's oldest burial sites, as well as hundreds of small ring forts. There are more than seventy burial tombs in the Burren, the most spectacular perhaps being the Poulnabrone. These tombs are mostly made up of limestone slabs set on their side to support an even larger slab, which sits on top, forming a large stone table effect. Don't spend too much time, however, pondering the dead here or you may miss the opportunity to spot the exceedingly rare Burren Green Moth.

You will need to look closely for the pretty little creature, as this is its only habitation in Britain and Ireland. The Burren Green has a wingspan of about 40 millimetres. Its head and the frontal part of its body, along with its front wings, are light green and have a couple of soft white spots. When it is not flying, it can hardly be seen, as it sits, wings folded, among the green vegetation of the area.

Also found here and nowhere else in Ireland, is the slow worm. This interesting creature is often mistaken for a snake (of which there are none in Ireland) but is actually a brown legless lizard. The slow worm is, as its name suggests, rather slow (and

can be easily caught) as it slithers across the limestone rocks of the area. It can grow to 50 centimetres in length and is perfectly harmless to humans because it is not poisonous, unlike some snakes. Look out for it, as it lies on the warm rocks in the sun during summer. Here, it seeks to draw heat from both the sun and the rocks as it is, like most reptiles, cold-blooded. Please don't, however, tread on one or harm them in any way, as they are rare and protected in both Britain and Ireland.

If you really want to go in for extreme adventure, a trip north to Donegal Bay should easily set your heart racing. Donegal Bay is Ireland's largest bay and it is here you will find cliffs that are just as impressive as the mighty Cliffs of Moher, for Donegal Bay is home to some of the highest cliffs in Europe, as they tower over 600 metres above the sea below (that is three times higher than the Cliffs of Moher)! These form the edge of Slieve League Mountain, where its western slopes have, over the years, been devoured by the strength of the sea. If you have a head for heights, why not take the aptly named One Man's Path: a narrow twisting path right across the mountain's summit, which affords one of the best walks in the whole of Ireland, as well as the most spectacular views of these breathtaking cliffs from a dizzying height?

Ireland is not just a land of green pasture but a place of upland mountain ranges which, although not as rugged or wild as the Highlands of Scotland, will still inspire those in search of adventure. Ireland's highest mountain, Carrantuohill, is found in County Kerry. This impressive mountain rises to 1,040 metres and is part of the strangely named Macgillycuddy's Reeks (translated Black Stacks) that stretches for 19 kilometres along the south-western tip of Ireland.

Further north, stretching out below Londonderry, are the more famous but less rugged Sperrin Mountains. However, perhaps most famous of all, are the beautiful and mysterious Mountains of Mourne in County Down. These mountains were made famous by Irish songwriter Percy French's popular song 'Where the Mountains of Mourne flow down to the sea', which has been recorded by many famous singers. Here you will find the beautiful coastal town of Newcastle, bordered by the Irish Sea to its east and the majestic Mountains of Mourne rising spectacularly to its southwest. The highest peak is Slieve Donard. However, further south is the impressive conical-shaped Slieve Binnion, which just begs to be climbed.

Amid this area of outstanding natural beauty you will also find the lonely and yet strangely magnetic Silent Valley, formed by building a dam across the River Kilkeel as it flows through the mountains. The resulting reservoir provides water for the great city of Belfast.

Lastly, in County Sligo, you will find the beautiful Knocknarea Mountain, made from limestone and rising to just over 309 metres. This is unusual in shape as it has limestone cliffs, woodland areas, as well as a striking curved profile. Then, there is the even more striking Ben Bulben. This is almost a miniature version of the famous Table Mountain in South Africa. It is most unusual as it has grass growing halfway up its sides, from which point the giant rock seems to have almost been pushed through the green to dominate the top half of the mountain. Unlike most mountains and hills, Ben Bulben is not rounded or peaked at the top but almost perfectly flat, making it resemble, from a distance, a giant solid table.

Travel north into County Antrim and you will come across Slemish Mountain or Slieve Mish. This looks remarkably similar to Ben Bulben, as it is more of an unusually-shaped hill than a proper mountain. Slemish is actually the plug of an extinct volcano and it stands in contrast to the rather flat farming land all around it. Depending from which direction you look, it can appear flat-topped or rounded but always very inviting, as you watch the sheep grazing on its slopes and the buzzards circling high above.

There are many mountains mentioned in the Bible. However, the most important to believers in the Lord Jesus, is a hill that sits just outside the City of Jerusalem. This hill is called Calvary and is where the Lord Jesus was crucified. It is given the name Calvary only once in the whole of the Bible. 'And when they were come to the place which is called Calvary, there they crucified him' (Luke 23:33). Why don't you look this important reference up in your own Bible?

This hill is also called Golgotha, which means the place of a skull. It could refer to the fact that people were taken there to die or, that from a certain angle, the hill actually looks like a human skull. It was here, on this hill that God dealt with sin, once and for all by providing his own Son as our substitute. 'For Christ also hath once suffered for sins, the just for the unjust that he might bring us to God' (1 Peter 3:18). Yes, the hill Calvary is so very precious to Christians; however, God's Son, the Lord Jesus, is more so, for the Bible states: 'Unto you therefore which believe he is precious' (1 Peter 2:7).

THINGS TO SEE AND DO:

- Atlantic Edge Visitor Centre, Cliffs of Moher, County Clare. This state of the art eco-friendly grass-covered underground visitor centre is just full of wonderful displays, images and information about the cliffs and more!
- O'Brien's Tower, Cliffs of Moher. This tower stands almost at the centre of the cliffs and is open to the public who want to get up close and personal with the cliffs and the amazing views the tower provides.
- The Burren Centre, Kilfenora, County Clare. This informative visitor centre has an informative exhibition on the area, shows films and has a coffee shop for mum and dad!

Towers, Turrets and Towns

Ireland has plenty of towers, turrets and towns. In fact, you can hardly stop in any town without coming across, somewhere nearby, an old fortification of a castle or tower of some shape, size or description.

Ireland is famous for its unusual and interesting round towers. At some time as you travel through this green and fertile land, you should be able to see at least one of Ireland's sixty-five round towers. Strange to relate, no one has yet fully discovered their original purpose. Many are associated with monasteries and so may have had some religious significance; however, the most likely explanation is that they were built as some form of lookout post or defence position. There is no doubt about it, though, that they are eye-catching, with their narrow profiles and pointed roofs.

The capitals Belfast and Dublin, as well as the smaller towns of Cork and Limerick, each have a castle and a story to tell.

It's the in thing these days to be called 'cool', so how about a visit to Coole Castle, just outside Enniskillen, in County Fermanagh? This must have been the coolest place to live in all of Ireland, because King George IV had bedrooms designed there to his specification! There is also the brilliant museum at nearby Enniskillen Castle. No owner really settled for too long at Coole, as it was continually fought over and occupied by different victors, until another would-be owner came along and took it over by strength. Today, you can view a whole host of military paraphernalia, bringing the history of this castle and region alive.

In visiting Dublin City, a trip to Dublin Castle is a must for anyone interested in history, if only to gaze at the magnificent Record Tower, which dates back as far as AD 1228. This was originally one of four towers placed at the four corners of the castle's square courtyard. Each of these four towers was given a strange name. One of them was Powder Tower, oddly enough used to store gunpowder! Sadly, much of the castle was destroyed by a great and destructive fire in 1673. However, the Record Tower to the southeast of the castle survived both the fire and subsequent demolition work that resulted. Perhaps one of its saving factors was its great strength, having walls over four

metres thick. No wonder this tower was used in the past as a prison for high security prisoners.

A wonderful verse in the Bible states something of the greatness of God and the protection he gives to those who trust in him. 'The Lord is my rock, and my fortress, and my deliverer; my God, my strength, in whom I will trust; my buckler, and the horn of my salvation, and my high tower' (Psalm 18:1). Wow! Just look at all those descriptions of God's strength and power. Those of us who are saved know that when times of great trial or difficulties come, we can tell God about them in prayer and he will support and shelter us through them all. What a wonderful promise this is to us in the great path of life. 'For thou hast been a shelter for me and a strong tower from the enemy' (Psalm 61:3). 'The name of the Lord is a strong tower: the righteous runneth into it and is safe' (Proverbs 18:10).

Travel up to the north coast between Portrush and Bushmills and you will come to the hauntingly mysterious Dunluce Castle. Dunluce sits in one of the most spectacular settings of any castle in the world, positioned high above the mighty roar of the Atlantic Ocean. Cut into the rock hundreds of metres below is Mermaid's Cave, which runs under the castle and helps to make the old ruins a place full of history and adventure. It was here that tragedy was to strike in 1639, when the rock supporting the castle kitchen suddenly gave way, casting the whole kitchen area including cooks and servants down the sheer cliff to perish in the sea below!

Surely the most impressive and complete castle in Ireland, however, must be St John's or Limerick Castle, sitting on the picturesque River Shannon in the beautiful city of Limerick. The castle boasts a five-sided wall with wonderful corner towers that were built for strength around AD 1210 during the reign of King John. The gatehouse is almost as interesting as the castle, with its double-towered grand entrance.

During what became known as the Irish Rebellion in 1641, when the native Irish sought unsuccessfully to take power from the British rulers, Limerick Castle became a refuge for those sympathetic to the British government. Here they were besieged in the castle by Irish forces who, not having any means available to storm the stronghold, gradually dug away at the foundations of one of the walls, with the intention of weakening them. Those sheltering inside surrendered just before the walls finally collapsed.

A trip down to County Waterford will bring you to Lismore Castle which, despite its grandeur, is sadly not open to the public. This castle, too, was built by King John, this time overlooking the River Blackwater and dwarfing the town of Lismore. Sir Walter Raleigh purchased the castle in 1589 but sold it to the First Earl of Cork in 1602, apparently without ever having lived there; despite the fact that Sir Walter was the mayor of the nearby town of Youghal in 1588 and 1589. His house, Myrtle Grove, still stands in the town. It is said that it was around here that Sir Walter also planted the first potatoes to be grown in Europe. Oh, and by the way, next time you are enjoying your chemistry lesson, think of Lismore Castle, for it was here that Robert Boyle the 'Father of Modern Chemistry' was born in 1627.

Run Aground

The *SS Great Britain* was not only the world's first propeller-driven steam ship but also the first iron-hulled ship ever to be built. At the time of its launch, by Prince Albert in Bristol on 19th July 1843, the *SS Great Britain* was the largest and most advanced passenger liner in the world. The ship's radical new design had been drawn up by the renowned designer, Isambard Kingdom Brunel, who was convinced that iron-hulled, steam-powered, propeller-driven ships were the future of seafaring. The ship weighed 3,675 tonnes, was nearly 100 metres long and over 15 metres wide. In fact it was so big that part of the harbour had to be dismantled in Bristol to allow the giant vessel out to sea!

The *SS Great Britain* was a huge success, traversing the world on thirty-two occasions and travelling over one million kilometres! The ship, however, was nearly lost in 1846 when she ran aground in Dundrum Bay, just north of Newcastle on the County Down coast. The *SS Great Britain* was bound for New York from Liverpool when the near disaster struck. The ship's captain, James Hosken, using out-of-date charts, mistook the St John's Point Lighthouse in Northern Ireland (which had only been built two years before and was not on his charts) for the Chicken Rock Lighthouse, on the Isle of Man. As he attempted to turn on to a northerly course to head out into the Atlantic Ocean across the top of Ireland, he found himself stuck fast on the treacherous sands of Dundrum Bay. The majority of passengers were, amazingly enough, able to climb off the ship at low tide and walk across the beach to safety.

Not wanting to lose his fantastic ship, Brunel travelled to Northern Ireland and wasted no time in seeking a way, to firstly protect the ship and then to refloat it. It was not an easy operation and cost £34,000, a vast amount of money in those days. Through Brunel's steadfast determination and perseverance, however, the *SS Great Britain* was refloated in August 1847, nearly a year after it ran aground. It went on to active service in one form or another for a further eighty-six years!

In 1933, she was abandoned in the Falkland Islands and left to rot away. Thankfully, however, in 1970 the ship was salvaged by those who realised its important place in history. The *SS Great Britain* was brought 12,875 kilometres across the Atlantic Ocean sitting forlornly upon a pontoon towed by a tug to her home port of Bristol. Here she was restored over many years and can now be seen in the original dry dock in which she was built.

What a wonderful reminder this great old iron ship is to us of what the Lord Jesus can do for us as we sail the sea of life. He can lift us off the sands of sin that hold us fast and then restore us into fellowship with God. At the end of our life he will then bring us safely to heaven; for the Bible records: 'He bringeth them unto their desired haven' (Psalm 107:30).

The 172 metre long, 13,510 tonne 'Laurentic' was operated by the White Star Line, the company that owned *Titanic!* The *Laurentic* worked the Liverpool–Canadian route and was a ship that became involved in one of the longest police chases in history! In 1909 Chief Inspector Walter Drew of Scotland Yard was in charge of one of the world's most interesting and intriguing murder investigations that resulted in a pursuit involving two ships across the Atlantic Ocean. Dr Hawley Crippen, after callously murdering his wife in London, was attempting to flee Britain. He caught the passenger ship *Montrose* intending to 'disappear' to Canada and hopefully literally 'get away with murder'! However, due to the great publicity surrounding the case, the captain of the ship he was travelling on recognised the fleeing Crippen and was able to inform the British authorities. Chief Inspector Drew quickly boarded the much larger and faster *Laurentic* which sailed for Canada a couple of days later and set off in pursuit of the wanted man. Due to greater speed of the *Laurentic* over the *Montrose,* Inspector Drew arrived in Canada ahead of Dr Crippen and was able to arrest him before he landed on Canadian soil! Crippen was brought back to London and eventually convicted of his wife's cruel murder. He was hanged at Pentonville Prison, London in 1910.

During the First World War on 25th January 1917 as the *Laurentic* was leaving Lough Swilly in County Donegal, she struck two German-laid mines and quickly sank claiming the lives of 354 of the 475 persons on board. At the time of her sinking, she was also carrying over £5 million worth of gold. This cargo was considered so valuable that over the next seven years Royal Navy divers made over 5,000 trips to the wreck site recovering almost ninety-nine per cent of the ships rich contents.

Dr Crippen discovered that the price for sin has to be paid and that it is very high! Maybe he really thought he would get away with murder. However, the Bible warns; 'Be sure your sin will find you out' (Numbers 32:23). However big or small your sin is, God still knows about it. The good news of the gospel is that the punishment for each sin has been paid by someone else, God's Son, the Lord Jesus Christ. The Bible says, 'But God commendeth his love toward us in that while we were yet sinners Christ died for us' (Romans 5:8). Thankfully, it goes on to say, 'Christ died for our sins...was buried....and rose again' (1 Corinthians 15:3-4). The Lord Jesus not only died to save us, but rose from the dead to keep us and offers a life far more satisfying than any amount of wealth this world has to offer, even the £5 million of gold rescued from the wreck of the *Laurentic*.

THINGS TO SEE AND DO:

- *SS Great Britain*, Great Western Dockyard, Bristol, England, BS1 6TY. See and explore the actual ship, now restored and resting in the dry dock in which she was built nearly 200 years ago!

Rivers and Rocks

The River Shannon is not just the longest river in Ireland but the longest river in both Britain and Ireland. It commences in the Cuilcagh Mountains of County Fermanagh, Northern Ireland, before winding its way down through thirteen counties of the Emerald Isle, on its 386 kilometre journey to the sea. It finally flows out into the wild Atlantic Ocean just south of the city of Limerick.

According to legend, the river is named after Sionan, an unfortunate lady who caught salmon from a certain well. The story goes that berries from an overhanging rowan tree had fallen into this well and been eaten by the salmon, giving them their distinctive red appearance and the wisdom to be able to return to their original breeding grounds each year. Ladies were forbidden to catch and eat salmon from this well and, when the unfortunate Sionan disobeyed, a torrent of water flooded out of the well, carrying the poor, helpless girl away to the sea in the west. The legend continues that the salmon still come up the river and whisper Sionan's name! A trip by boat along the length of this wonderful river would indeed be an interesting and exciting way to discover the history and wildlife of this fascinating country.

Perhaps the prettiest river in Ireland is its second longest, the Barrow, as it winds its way down the south eastern side of the country. Along its 192 kilometre length, you can experience twenty-three working Victorian locks that lift or lower boats along the river. The river bank of the Barrow is a haven for wildlife with its reed beds and secluded shrubs, bushes and grasslands.

If you like old buildings, hidden tunnels, high towers and history that go back as far as records began, then make for the famous Rock of Cashel, in County Tipperary. This mysterious location is often the highlight of many a visitor's tour of Ireland and is also known by the name of 'St Patrick's Rock'. It was here, in AD 450, that St Patrick converted King Aenghus to Christianity. Legend records that, during the king's baptismal service, Patrick accidentally stabbed the king through the foot with his bishop's staff. Unbelievably, the king remained upright and silent, thinking this was a part of the service, as he listened to Patrick preaching!

It was from this spot that Munster was ruled in the early years of the 4th and 5th centuries. Following Patrick's visit, the building of the cathedral was commenced, along with a smaller chapel and a 28 metre round tower, to serve as a lookout post. Here you can explore these wonderful and interesting ruins as you travel back in time over 1,500 years.

No visit to Ireland would be complete without a visit to the Giant's Causeway on the North Antrim coast. Once described as the eighth wonder of the world, this breathtaking area of cliffs and hexagonal (six-sided) stone pillars, is indeed a place to ponder and marvel. Here, after a brisk walk downhill from the visitor centre, you can sit on one of the over 40,000 stone pillars and view the sea as it crashes in over this unique rocky landscape.

The rock columns rise to a maximum height of 100 metres and then drop until you have much shorter ones on the water's edge and even smaller ones that are below the water's surface.

People, who do not believe in God, say that these unique rocks are millions of years old and yet the Bible speaks about the great worldwide flood of Noah's day, when it not only rained but 'the fountains of the deep were broken up' (Genesis 7:11). This expression would suggest volcanic activity and, here at the Giant's Causeway, you will find seven distinct lava flows, caused during great upheavals of the earth, as the lava was forced through its crust before being cooled by the large amounts of water above.

The Giant's Causeway is a great reminder of the days of Noah when God judged the world with a great flood, and should therefore remind us of another day of judgement that the Bible

warns is coming, when God will judge the world that rejected his Son, not this time with water, but with fire. 'The Lord Jesus shall be revealed from heaven with his mighty angels, in flaming fire taking vengeance on them that know not God, and that obey not the gospel of our Lord Jesus Christ' (2 Thessalonians 1:7-8).

THINGS TO SEE AND DO:
- Giant's Causeway, Causeway Road, Bushmills County Antrim, BT57 8SU – state-of-the-art visitor centre, with facts and figures about the causeway, as well as the story of Finn MacCool! Here, you can explore the wonderful causeway columns, as well as look out for Finn's boot, grandma, harp, and organ!

Starvation

By the mid 1800s, potatoes were the mainstay of the Irishman's diet. The most popular crops were called 'Horse Potatoes' or 'Lumpers', as they would grow almost anywhere and always gave a bumper harvest. These potatoes could be dug up in August and kept and used right through the year until the following summer, when the new crop was planted. At this time, the diet changed to oats, for a couple of months, until the next crop of potatoes was ready to be dug up. The majority of the population were very poor, and managed to live almost totally on this simple fare. However, disaster was in store.

When the potato crop was harvested in 1845, the plants' leaves above ground looked normal but, once the potatoes were cut open, it was discovered that the insides were absolutely rotten and totally inedible. This fungus was known as the Potato Blight and it quickly spread throughout the country resulting, during the next five years, in the loss of nearly two million lives! The British government, which ruled Ireland at that time, were divided on how to help. Some politicians wanted to send more aid and resources, but others were so heartless that they believed this famine was a great judgement by God on a rebellious land and therefore the people should be left to die.

All across Ireland, the dreadful scenes of hunger, dying and death were repeated. Families died together of starvation in their own homes and, instead of being buried, their houses were pulled down on top of their bodies to form a makeshift grave. The population, in desperation, sought out the local wildlife and went out to trap rabbits, hedgehogs, foxes, badgers, mice and even rats to feed themselves. Within two years the wildlife of Ireland, like the people was decimated, as a result of hunting by poor people just struggling to stay alive.

Due to the population's malnutrition, disease and fever rapidly set in, killing even more than the terrible lack of food. Typhus and black fever were illnesses spread by fleas, carried by the living and passed on from one to another. Sickness and dysentery were commonplace with hundreds dying in the most terrible ways imaginable.

The conditions in Ireland being dire and the British government of the day seemingly reluctant to assist, resulted in mass emigration. Many embarked on ships to make an horrendous journey across 4,828 kilometres of Atlantic Ocean hoping to start a new life in America. Many of the ships which set sail were overcrowded and did not carry enough food or fresh water for everyone on board. Some were not seaworthy and sank without trace before ever reaching America.

For those who took to the sea, the crossing was nightmarish, on what came to be called 'Famine Ships' or maybe more correctly 'Coffin Ships', as so many died whilst seeking to make the journey! Those that survived the crossing and finally arrived in America were put into makeshift slums, in which, once again, starvation and disease were constant companions. Many Americans resented these Irish immigrants and there were protests and even violence against them.

During this time in Ireland, most of the poorest people rented their homes and land from landlords (rich people, who usually lived in large houses and had lots of land). When the poor were unable to pay their rent, many of these callous landlords threw them out of their homes and off their land. This left thousands of families starving, penniless and now homeless, having no shelter, apart from bushes and ditches.

The British government, eventually shamed into action, set up soup kitchens in some of the larger towns, in which crowds had to queue for hours for a bowl of soup, which was little more than warm water. Many kitchens were too far for those in the more rural areas to reach, so they just continued getting weaker and thinner!

Queen Victoria gave £5,000 from her own wealth, to help the dire situation but, such was the anti-British resentment at their lack of aid, the story went around that the queen had only given £5! Sadly, with the best of intentions, Queen Victoria made a trip to Ireland in 1849, to see personally the sad situation in the country. She hoped that her visit would improve morale in the country, but it seemingly only caused more resentment, as the poor dressed in their rags came to see the queen dressed in her finery. The cost of her visit could well have been used to save many hundreds of lives by providing food to the starving.

Meanwhile, the government again sought to help by getting the poor (including women and children) to work, making roads across the land. These roads had no plans, were not really needed and often led nowhere in particular. In exchange, the government paid the workers a pittance, which just about kept them able to buy a little more food (if it was available) than before. Many had to endure one of the worst recorded winters in Irish history, as they built seemingly useless roads in driving snow and freezing conditions. Hundreds of workers fell down, dying in the extreme conditions and were buried where they fell.

After five years of famine and crop failures, the blight ended in 1850 and the first good potato harvest for five years was gathered in. Sadly, by this time, over 1.5 million people had died and over one million had left the Emerald Isle, hoping for a better life in America.

The Christian, just like anyone else, needs physical food in order to stay alive. However, they also need a good diet of spiritual food on a daily basis, in order to resist temptation, grow as a Christian and become more like the Lord Jesus. They get this food from the Bible, by reading it daily and meditating upon what it says. Job was a great man in the Bible and, despite going through a great trial, was able to say: 'I have esteemed the words of his (God's) mouth more than my necessary food' (Job 23:12). Job actually said that the spiritual food of God's Word was more important to him than the food he ate in order to live.

Another man in the Bible said, 'Thy word have I hid in my heart that I might not sin against thee' (Psalm 119:11). If we daily spend

time reading God's Word and allowing him to speak to us, as well as seeking to memorise as much of the Bible as we can, we will find that God will give us just the right promises, encouragements and help we require, exactly when we need it. Have you read your Bible today?

THINGS TO SEE AND DO:
- The Irish National Famine Museum, Strokestown Park, Strokestown, County Roscommon. This museum is dedicated to the Irish potato famine with lots of exhibits and fascinating facts. It is also worth looking round the stately home and gardens.
- Jeanie Johnson Famine Ship, Custom House Quay, Dublin. This is a genuine famine ship and exhibition to show what conditions were like for those who chose to leave Ireland for America on ships like these.
- Donaghmore Famine Workhouse Museum, Donaghmore, Portlaoise, Co Laois. A unique tour can be taken around a genuine famine workhouse.

Saint Patrick

Saint Patrick, the patron saint of Ireland, was indeed a real person, although trying to separate fact from fiction about his life is hard to do nearly 1,600 years after his death. Patrick was actually born in AD 389 and, believe it or not, was born in Wales! It seems that Patrick was brought up in a relatively well-to-do home, which employed servants and had a good deal of land. Patrick was captured, when aged about sixteen, by Irish raiders and taken to Ireland, where he was made to work as a slave attending sheep, possibly around the Slemish Mountain in County Antrim. After six years, he managed to escape, it is thought, firstly by travelling south and then by sea, back to his native Wales.

In one of only two authentic letters from Patrick to have survived, called *Confessions*, he states, 'I am Patrick, a sinner.' He goes on to recount how the Lord had saved him: 'The Lord opened the understanding of my unbelieving heart that I might recall my sins and turn with all my heart to the Lord my God'.

It seems that about thirty years after returning from Ireland, he believed that God was calling him to go back and preach the gospel, in the land where he had been a prisoner so many years before. Patrick was not disobedient and, once more, travelled by sea to Ireland, there to commence his heavenly calling by telling the natives about the Lord Jesus.

The second of Patrick's surviving letters was written to a man by the name of Coroticus. This cruel landowner had already killed a number of Christians and had also captured others with the intention of selling them into slavery. This was too much for the saintly Patrick, who wrote an open letter to the wicked man commanding him and his servants to repent of their wickedness before eternal judgement overtook them. He finishes his letter by stating, 'Let every God-fearing man know they are enemies of me and of Christ my God, for whom I am an ambassador.'

There are many myths and legends too, which have built up over time, around the life and times of St Patrick and, of course, the whole of Ireland remembers this giant of a man, on March 17th each year – St Patrick's Day.

Legend states that it was Patrick who banished all snakes from Ireland, after being attacked by them whilst undertaking a forty-day fast, on top of Croagh Patrick in County Mayo. Although there are no snakes in Ireland today, it is possible that this legend was built up as a result of Patrick bringing Christianity to Ireland. The Christian faith rapidly replaced the dark, false pagan religions, which actually had serpents as their main symbols.

Each year, thousands remember the banishing of the snakes, on the last Sunday in July (known as Reek Sunday). On that day, many people make a pilgrimage to the 762 metre Croagh Patrick, in order to climb its scree path. Hundreds actually climb in their bare feet, and this event attracts in excess of 20,000 people. The procession is usually led by the Archbishop of Tuam, who then conducts a service on the mountain's summit.

Another tradition built up around the life of Patrick, is his use of a three-sided clover (known in Ireland as a shamrock) in order to show the great biblical truth of the Trinity. The simple picture of the three identical leaves in the clover represents the three equal persons of the Trinity, each of whom is God. These are: God the Father, who loves each one; God the Son, The Lord Jesus Christ, who died on the cross for us; God the Holy Spirit, who convicts us of our sin and our need to trust the Lord Jesus Christ as our Saviour!

When we repent of our sins and trust the Lord Jesus as our Saviour, two things will immediately happen. Firstly, we will have a desire to serve God and work for him every day. Secondly, this will result in us never being the same again, as the old sinful things which used to occupy our time and effort will be cast out. The Bible states, 'If any man be in Christ, he is a new creature: old things are passed away; behold all things are become new' (2 Corinthians 5:17). Are you saved? If you are, are you willing to serve God every day of your life like Patrick, or are there still things you need to chase out of your life, in order to be the Christian you should be?

THINGS TO SEE AND DO:

- Look out for the St Patrick's Trail in County Down. Follow this and you will discover museums, churches and other fascinating places connected with Patrick and the early rise of Christianity in Ireland.

Safe and Sound!

Guglielmo Marconi does not sound like an Irish name and, it isn't. He was born in Italy in 1874 but, by the age of twenty, had already set up a very impressive workshop in his parents' home and had commenced various experiments transmitting sound (or radio) waves over increasingly large distances, without wires. With his parents' financial backing, he contacted the ministry of telegraphs in Rome, looking for more extensive government funding into his work in wireless communications. The minister, upon reading Marconi's letter, wrote across it: 'To the insane asylum' and never even bothered to reply!

This led Marconi to move to England at the age of twenty-one, where he received great interest from the British Post Office. He conducted a series of experiments over both land and sea, sending a series of Morse code messages (made up of dots and dashes) over increasing distances. On 6th July 1898, he visited Ballycastle on the North Antrim Coast in Northern Ireland and made the first radio transmission on Irish soil, between radio transmitters and receivers he had set up in the East Lighthouse on Rathlin Island and Kenmara House in Ballycastle. A monument can be seen at the harbour to mark the event. Marconi rented White Lodge Cottage, near the town, for a short period whilst conducting his experiments.

This was not to be Marconi's only success on Irish soil. As his experimentation grew, he was soon able to transmit messages, using huge antennas, from Cornwall to Newfoundland in Canada; a distance of well over 4,828 kilometres. He then set up a wireless station at Clifden in Galway, from which, on 17th October 1907 he was able to establish the first regular Trans-Atlantic radio service.

In 1912, Marconi's invention came fully into its own, when distress messages were picked up from the sinking *Titanic*, in America and by other ships, following its collision with the iceberg on 14th April 1912. This means of communication alerted the ship *Carpathia* to the *Titanic's* plight, thus allowing it to steam to the rescue of the 705 passengers who had made it safely into the lifeboats.

Another highlight for the Italian inventor occurred in March 1919, when the first ever broadcast by voice was made from the Ballybunion Marconi station in County Kerry. This station had seven masts, the tallest stretching 153 metres into the sky. Here one of Marconi's engineers, Mr W. T. Ditcham, picked up the microphone to his 2.5 kilowatt transmitter and said, 'Hello America. Hello, Picken. Can you hear me? This is Ditcham of Chelmsford, England, speaking from Ballybunion, Ireland.' The man in America was able to hear the transmission, but not able to answer due to only having a receiving set. This short message, however, from the west coast of Ireland was the commencement of radio broadcasting around the world.

Today, we can listen to the radio, communicate using walkie-talkies or mobile phones and even see pictures on a television screen, thanks, in great measure, to the amazing work of the Italian inventor with Irish connections, Guglielmo Marconi!

It's good to know that, as Christians, we can speak to God about anything, anytime, anywhere! We do not need a mobile phone or any other type of transmitting or receiving equipment, to get through. The Bible says, 'Be careful for nothing; but in everything by prayer and supplication with thanksgiving let your requests be made known unto God' (Philippians 4:6). It's great to be able to speak to God but this verse also speaks about 'thanksgiving' so don't forget to always be thankful to him.

Being surrounded by sea, Ireland has a large number of lighthouses — just over 100 in total. Many of these have great stories to tell, are in interesting places or have unusual names. Some of them are on small offshore islands which are so remote, the only way to reach them safely is by helicopter, whilst others sit in some of the most breathtaking and spectacular settings of any lighthouse in the world. Let's take a quick tour of some of the Irish lighthouses.

The most southerly lighthouse is at Crookhaven (another place from which Senor Marconi used to send and receive wireless transmissions) right at the southwestern tip of County Cork. The most northerly lighthouse is not on the mainland at all but on the wild rugged island of Inishtrahull, which lies 10 kilometres northeast of Malin Head. Many ships have been wrecked in and around the dangerous waters of this island in the last two hundred years.

Although Inishtrahull is now no longer populated by humans, it is a place of real interest if you like wildlife. Offshore, you

may well see playful dolphins or porpoises, the occasional pod of passing killer whales or the regular sight of the giant but perfectly harmless basking shark with its huge open mouth, seeking to catch microscopic bits of plant life on which it feeds.

Off the southwestern point of County Cork, you will come across Bull Rock Lighthouse which sits on top of the 300 foot high island. Bull Rock is unusual, as it has a massive tunnel cut by the sea right through its middle. This cave is so big that it could accommodate a ship! The island is part of a group or a 'herd' of islands. The others are called The Cow, The Calf and The Heifer! Here, on the smaller and lower Calf Rock, you will find the remains of the first lighthouse to be put up in these dangerous waters. It was built of iron in 1862 and stood over 31 metres high. However, in February 1869 disaster struck during a fierce storm.

Seven men from the mainland, believing that the keepers' lives were in danger, set out on a rescue mission in an open boat. In reaching the lighthouse, they discovered the keepers to be in no immediate danger and so commenced the return journey to the safety of the shore. Sadly, the storm proved too much for the small rowing boat and all seven men were lost.

For those desiring to go up in the world, a trip west to Eagle Island Lighthouse might be the solution! This lighthouse sits on top of a 40 metre high cliff face off the west coast of County Mayo and is regularly buffeted by the wild and stormy Atlantic waves which crash around its shores. This place is so exposed to the power of the sea that a huge storm wall was built right along the cliff top of its most westerly edge, in order to protect the lighthouses and buildings.

Despite that, over the years, the two lighthouses which occupied this small rocky island, have taken a huge beating from the fierce Atlantic storms. The easternmost lighthouse collapsed during a storm after being taken out of commission in 1895 and its remains can still be seen still strewed across the island. Its more westerly sister was struck by a 68 metre wave in March 1861, which broke much of the glass and many of the lamps! So much water came into the tower that the keepers had to drill holes in the walls to drain it before they could reach and open the door!

As you enter New York harbour in America, you will pass the famous 'Statue of Liberty' as it stands proudly welcoming visitors to this mighty city. If you are entering Sligo Bay on the west coast of Ireland, you will pass the slightly less well known 'Metal Man' as he welcomes visitors to the Emerald Isle! Almost unbelievably, Metal Man is a lighthouse, sitting upon a 4.6 metre stone base above the dangerous Perch Rock. Metal Man is 3.7 metres high and apparently weighs an unbelievable 6 tonnes. He stands, dressed in a blue jacket with white trousers, holding out an outstretched right arm, which points along the safe passage through the bay to the town of Sligo. Just in front of him sits the light which, if lined up with another on Oyster Island further up channel, will show safe passage to ships travelling through the bay. Apparently, the crew of a large foreign steamship were terrified in 1926 when, as they entered the bay in dense fog, a giant man suddenly appeared alongside the ship, causing them to flee in terror!

If we are Christians, we are to be like lighthouses. The Lord Jesus said, 'I am the Light of the World, he that followeth me shall not walk in darkness, but shall have the light of life' (John 8:12). The Lord also told his followers on another occasion, 'Ye are the light of the world' (Matthew 5:14) and then added: 'Let your light so shine before men, that they may see your good works, and glorify your father which is in heaven' (Matthew 5:16). It follows we should not be ashamed to show, by our life and words, that we belong to the Lord Jesus, by letting our light shine before others. Who knows, perhaps we may be used by God, to stop someone from wrecking their lives on the jagged rocks of sin?

THINGS TO SEE AND DO

- Mizan Head Signal Station Visitor Centre, Goleen, West Cork. This is a most interesting centre with the history of Marconi's first transatlantic wireless communications, as well as that of the Lighthouse and other facts about the area.
- Inishowen Maritime Museum and Planetarium, Old Coastguard Station, Greencastle, County Donegal. This is an extremely interesting museum to do with all things maritime, from lighthouses to shipwrecks, to wartime experiences.

Sink the Bismarck!

In May 1941, the German navy unleashed upon the high seas, its new monster battleship, *Bismarck*. The *Bismarck* was a 45,359 tonne, 250 metre monster of a ship which, humanly speaking, the Royal Navy had little chance of stopping. It had a top speed of 30 knots and a company of over 2,200 men! It could fire its massive shells over 26 kilometres, making it a formidable opponent to the allies. On 5th May, Adolph Hitler, the German leader, boarded and inspected the ship prior to ordering it out to sea on its first operation.

On 23rd May, after leaving Norway and sailing out into the Atlantic Ocean, the *Bismarck* and a smaller battle cruiser, *Prinz Eugen*, encountered the British battleships, *Hood* and *Prince of Wales*. At that time HMS *Hood* was the largest battleship that the Royal Navy had and *Prince of Wales* was so new it still had workmen on board seeking to complete its fitting out! The four ships engaged each other in battle at a distance of about 24 kilometres. After an eight-minute confrontation, *Bismarck's* fifth salvo hit *Hood* in her rear ammunition store, causing a massive explosion. The *Hood* broke in two, sinking almost instantaneously and leaving only three survivors of its nearly 1,500 men. The

Prince of Wales was so badly damaged in the confrontation she had to retreat to safety.

With the loss of the pride of the Royal Navy after such a short exchange with the *Bismarck*, the race was on to find and sink this powerful ship before it reached the vital convoys of ships bringing much needed food supplies from the U.S. to the U.K. Winston Churchill, the British Prime Minister, gave the widely broadcasted and uncoded order to 'Sink the *Bismarck*!'

God, in his Word, gives an even more important command than that given by Britain's wartime Prime Minister. God's command concerns, not the sinking of a ship, but the salvation of our souls. This clear instruction is that we, 'Repent and believe the gospel' (Mark 1:15). To repent means to be sorry for our sin and want to be rid of it. We then need to believe the gospel (good news) that God loves us and the Lord Jesus died and rose again to save us.

The *Bismarck* managed to lose its pursuing Royal Navy ships and start on a course for Brest in occupied France, where it could receive both air cover and the protection of the German navy's fleet of U-Boat submarines. A desperate search by British ships and aircraft was conducted to locate and sink this monster of the seas.

On 26th May, three days after the *Bismarck's* defeat of *Hood*, a Catalina flying boat, operating out of Loch Erne in County Fermanagh and flown by Flying Officer Dennis Briggs and a U.S. Navy Pilot Leonard B. 'Tuck' Smith, spotted the *Bismarck* 1,288 kilometres away from Brest. The flying boats had been given permission, in a secret deal with the Republic of Ireland, to fly across their neutral airspace, in what became known as the 'Donegal Corridor'. This helped the aircraft to conserve fuel and increase their operating range.

The *Bismarck* immediately opened fire on the plane, causing minor damage. This did not stop the crew from informing the large British Naval Fleet in the area as to the *Bismarck's* position, allowing bi-winged 'Swordfish' aircraft from the nearby aircraft carrier *Ark Royal* to attack the German ship. Using torpedoes, these old-fashioned looking planes managed to cause serious damage to the battleship's rudder restricting her manoeuvrability. Amazingly, this attack was carried out without any loss of life to the pilots or crew involved. The *Bismarck* was left unable to steer herself and was still a considerable distance from the safety of other German forces. The Royal Navy ships were then able to close in on the stricken battleship. The next day, the *Bismarck* engaged in a fierce, but unequal, battle with the Royal Navy that lasted for nearly two hours. Shell after shell rained down upon the German ship which became a blazing wreck, before finally capsizing and sinking beneath the cold dark waters of the Atlantic Ocean. Tragically, only 114 survivors of the 2,200 German sailors on board when the *Bismarck* sailed were rescued from the freezing waters.

THINGS TO SEE AND DO:

- A trip to the Fermanagh Lakes is always a delightful experience as they are undoubtedly one of the most beautiful natural areas in Ireland. Stand on the shores of Loch Erne and imagine watching the Catalina flying boats taking off from the surface of the lake in search of the mighty *Bismarck*.
- If you want to go further a field a trip to Hakoy island near Tromso in Norway will reward you with a view of the final resting place of *Bismarck's* sister ship *Tirpitz'* which was finally sunk by RAF Lancaster bombers on 12th November 1944.

Waves and Caves

Surrounded by water as it is, Ireland has a very good surfing community, all eager to capitalize on the exciting breakers, which come crashing in around its shoreline. Nowadays surfers from the world over arrive on Ireland's green shores, looking for its golden sands and blue waves!

With its north, south and west shores facing the mighty Atlantic Ocean, it is not surprising that there really are some great places to take your board and catch a wave or two. The water temperature is actually warmest during autumn, which is also the best time to catch the biggest and best surfing waves Ireland's shoreline has to offer. Here, on the Atlantic-facing beaches, you can regularly find waves tumbling in which are in excess of 1.8 metres in height.

Surfing in Ireland is a relatively new sport, only really taking off in the 1960s. However, one surf-mad lad was catching waves at least a decade before that, and his name was Joe Roddy. Joe was the son of a lighthouse keeper and was brought up in Dundalk during the post war years, when materials were in short supply and surf boards non-existent. He was a resourceful young chap and set about making his own four-metre surf board, out of old tea chests covered in paint, taken from his father's lighthouse.

Surfboards were not his only invention. He made flippers from aluminium pipe, hammered into a triangular shape and attached to a pair of boots! He made goggles from an old gas mask and painted his old long john underwear with tar to form a makeshift wet-suit! How about that for innovation?

With such dedication and resourcefulness, Joe was soon up and surfing on his own giant home-made board. Those lounging on the beach soon looked on in awe and wonder, as this young man swept towards the beach, whilst standing on his half-submerged board. Eyes bulged and mouths opened, as he drew closer to the shore, before jumping off into the shallows. As far as can be discerned, Joe was Ireland's first surfer!

It was, however, in the 1960s that the sport really took off around Ireland's coast. In these early years, surfers usually made their own boards of plywood or, better still, marine ply coupled with some form of insulation stuck to it. Many were made of balsa wood. However, news was filtering in that American surfers were using new 'fibre glass' boards and soon these were appearing on the beaches of Ireland. In the mid sixties, the Surf Club of Ireland was formed and surfing in Ireland had really rolled in!

So where are Ireland's surfing hot spots?

You may hope to catch the odd 'freak' wave at County Cork's Castle Freak! This wonderfully remote area, on Ireland's south coast, catches some pretty big Atlantic rollers as they crash into the shore.

If you rush up north, Portrush has some pretty good surfing on both its east and west strands, and it affords the bonus of a spectacular location as you look out to the Skerries Islands, which lie just offshore.

If you visit the beach of Strandhill near Sligo, hopefully you will not stand still for too long, waiting for some good waves to come in! Here, you will find a vast beach, which can provide some really excellent and challenging conditions for even the most experienced surfer!

The Bible has a little to say about waves, often to show the power of our God: 'Thou rulest the raging of the sea: when the waves thereof arise thou stillest them' (Psalm 89:9). Another similar verse says, 'The Lord on high is mightier than the noise of many waters, yea, than the mighty waves of the sea'. (Psalm 93:4). Christians can always rest in the wonderful fact that whatever circumstances we find ourselves in, our God is far bigger and greater than them all!

Well, if maybe the sea is a bit too cold or rough and the weather is not as hot as you would hope, then you could always travel underground, to have a look at Ireland's wonderful hidden gems in its many cave systems.

A visit to Doolin Cave in County Clare, is a must if you want to view the largest stalactite in the Northern Hemisphere. Here, as you

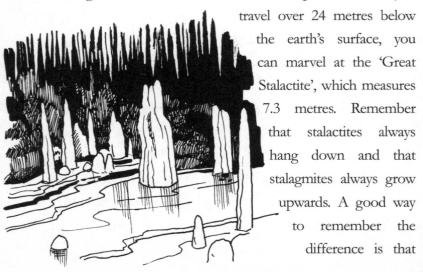

travel over 24 metres below the earth's surface, you can marvel at the 'Great Stalactite', which measures 7.3 metres. Remember that stalactites always hang down and that stalagmites always grow upwards. A good way to remember the difference is that a stalactite holds 'tight' onto the roof whereas stalagmites 'might' eventually grow up to meet a stalactite! The 'Great Stalactite' of Doolan was first discovered in 1952, but in those days could only be seen by a very few really experienced cavers. Now, you too, can explore the wonders of this cave system and marvel at God's unseen creation below ground.

In County Fermanagh, you will come across one of the longest cave systems in Britain and Ireland - Marble Arch Caves. These certainly live up to their claim to be some of Europe's finest show caves, as you move from one fascinating chamber to another, during your seventy-five minute tour. Not only do you walk but you can travel along a subterranean river, on special electrically-powered boats.

This whole system of caves goes 94 metres underground and has an incredible length of 11.5 kilometres. Sad to say, you will only get to see a fraction of this monster cavern on your visit. The caves were first explored by a French cave scientist in 1895 without the use of any electric lights. Stand still and try to imagine what it would have been like finding your way through the darkness with only the light of a candle or paraffin lamp to guide you. At the end of your tour, you finish with the Moses Walk, so named after Moses' leading the Children of Israel through the Red Sea. Here you take a short man-made path which leads you through an underground lake.

Take a trip by boat to Rathlin Island off Ballycastle in County Antrim and you will come across the famous Bruce's Cave. Here, you need to visit the cave under the East Lighthouse at Altacarry. Robert the Bruce fled to Rathlin, following defeat by the English in 1306. Legend records that Robert got inspiration to return to Scotland and fight the English again, by watching a spider weaving its intricate web, whilst hiding in this cave. He observed it trying to attach the web to the cave walls and failing, time and again. However, the spider never gave up and kept trying until, at last, it succeeded. Robert decided to follow the spider's example and returned to Scotland where, in 1314, he defeated the proud English King Edward at the Battle of Bannockburn, thus setting Scotland free from English rule.

There is a cave in the Bible that was visited by the Lord Jesus on one important occasion. In this cave lay the body of his friend, Lazarus, who had died. 'Jesus therefore again groaning in himself cometh to the grave. It was a cave, and a stone lay upon it' (John 11:38). Here, the Lord was going to perform perhaps his greatest recorded miracle. He was going to raise Lazarus to life, after he had been dead for four days! Simply by calling: 'Lazarus come forth' (John 11:43), the Lord gave him new life. Lazarus was one of three recorded people whom the Lord raised from the dead. However, three days after he died, the Lord himself rose alive from the dead. The Bible records that: 'Christ died for our sins....that he was buried and that he rose again the third day' (1 Corinthians 15:3-4). We can have absolute confidence in knowing that, because the Lord Jesus died and rose again and lives in heaven, he is more than able to give new and eternal life, to all who will come unto God, through him.

THINGS TO SEE AND DO:
- Doolin Cave, Doolin, County Clare. Go here to see the Great Stalactite, the biggest in the Northern Hemisphere.
- Marble Arch Caves, Marlbank, Florencecourt, County Fermanagh, BT92 1EW. Here, you can explore the various underwater passages with a guide, as well as take an electric boat ride along an underground river.
- Rathin Island, County Antrim. Take the ferry from Ballycastle and allow at least a day, to explore this famous and interesting offshore Island.

Emerald Isle Map

Emerald Isle Quiz

1. How did the 'Emerald Isle' get it's name?

2. What was the thirty-year period of unrest at the end of the last century known as?

3. What year did the first 'roll-on-roll-off' passenger ferry start sailing in British waters?

4. Why are most people in a wrong position with regard to God?

5. Who was the first person to fly an aeroplane over Ireland?

6. What was a 'Little Grey Fergie'?

7. Where was C.S. Lewis born?

8. What does C.S. Lewis depict in *The Chronicles of Narnia*?

9. What divides the city of Dublin in two?

10. What is the division between us and God?

11. Which building has the 'Door of Reconciliation'?

12. Where was Grace, the lady pirate, imprisoned?

13. Name two unusual games played in Ireland?

14. Name the famous ship built in Belfast which sank on its first voyage?

15. Where is the Giant's Causeway?

16. What is a slow worm?

17. What is the name of Ireland's highest mountain?

18. Why is Calvary important to believers in the Lord Jesus?

19. How long is the River Shannon?

20. Where do we get our spiritual food?

21. Where was St Patrick born?

22. What did St Patrick use to show the biblical truth of the Trinity?

23. What did Marconi do in 1898?

24. How many lighthouses does Ireland have?

25. What did Jesus say about himself in John 8:12?

26. How big is the 'Great Stalactite?

27. What cave did Jesus visit on one occasion?

Emerald Isle Answers

1. The predominant colour is green.

2. The Troubles.

3. 1947.

4. They don't realise that they have sin in their lives which separate them from God.

5. Harry Ferguson.

6. A type of tractor which allowed different tools to be easily attached.

7. Belfast.

8. The fight between good and evil.

9. River Liffey.

10. Our sin and guilt.

11. St Patrick's Cathedral, Dublin.

12. Limerick Castle.

13. Gaelic Football and Hurling.

14. The Titanic.

15. On the North Antrim coast.

16. A brown legless lizard.

17. Carrantuohill.

18. It's where Jesus died for our sin.

19. 386 kilometres.

20. The Bible.

21. Wales.

22. The Shramrock.

23. He made the first radio transmission on Irish soil.

24. Just over 100.

25. He called himself the Light of the World.

26. 7.3 metres.

27. The tomb of Lazarus.

About the Author

Originally from England, Robert Plant moved to Northern Ireland in 2010. He became a Christian aged sixteen through the witness of a friend at school.

In 1993 he left his job as a Safety Manager in a large construction firm to serve the Lord as a full time Christian Evangelist. Robert has written several articles for Christian periodicals and other publications. He is author of the Christian Focus title *Titanic – Ship of Dreams,* the story of preacher John Harper.

He travels extensively throughout the British Isles and conducts many series of Children's Meetings each year as well as scores of School assemblies. He has a desire to provide good readable material for children that will point them to the Bible as the authoritative and divinely inspired Word of God and to the Lord Jesus Christ the Son of God and only way of salvation. Robert, his wife Karen, and teenage daughter, Grace, reside on the North Antrim Coast from where they can see the cliffs of the Giant's Causeway.

The Adventures Series
An ideal series to collect

Have you ever wanted to visit the rainforest? Have you ever longed to sail down the Amazon river? Would you just love to go on Safari in Africa? Well these books can help you imagine that you are actually there.

Pioneer missionaries retell their amazing adventures and encounters with animals and nature. In the Amazon you will discover tree frogs, piranha fish and electric eels. In the Rainforest you will be amazed at the armadillo and the toucan. In the blistering heat of the African Savannah you will come across lions and elephants and hyenas. And you will discover how God is at work in these amazing environments.

African Adventures by Dick Anderson
ISBN 978-1-85792-807-5
Amazon Adventures by Horace Banner
ISBN 978-1-85792-440-4
Antarctic Adventures by Bartha Hill
ISBN 978-1-78191-135-8
Cambodian Adventures by Donna Vann
ISBN 978-1-84550-474-8
Emerald Isle Adventures by Robert Plant
ISBN 978-1-78191-136-5
Great Barrier Reef Adventures by Jim Cromarty
ISBN 978-1-84550-068-9
Himalayan Adventures by Penny Reeve
ISBN 978-1-84550-080-1
Kiwi Adventures by Bartha Hill
ISBN 978-1-84550-282-9
New York City Adventures by Donna Vann
ISBN 978-1-84550-546-2
Outback Adventures by Jim Cromarty
ISBN 978-1-85792-974-4
Pacific Adventures by Jim Cromarty
ISBN 978-1-84550-475-5
Rainforest Adventures by Horace Banner
ISBN 978-1-85792-627-9
Rocky Mountain Adventures by Betty Swinford
ISBN 978-1-85792-962-1
Scottish Highland Adventures by Catherine Mackenzie
ISBN 978-1-84550-281-2
Wild West Adventures by Donna Vann
ISBN 978-1-84550-065-8

CHRISTIAN FOCUS PUBLICATIONS

Christian Focus · Christian Heritage · CF4K · Mentor

Christian Focus Publications publishes books for adults and children under its four main imprints: Christian Focus, CF4K, Mentor and Christian Heritage. Our books reflect our conviction that God's Word is reliable and Jesus is the way to know him, and live for ever with him.

Our children's publication list includes a Sunday School curriculum that covers pre-school to early teens, and puzzle and activity books. We also publish personal and family devotional titles, biographies and inspirational stories that children will love.

If you are looking for quality Bible teaching for children then we have an excellent range of Bible stories and age-specific theological books.

From pre-school board books to teenage apologetics, we have it covered!

Find us at our web page:
www.christianfocus.com

CF4 •K
Because you're never
too young to know Jesus